# First World War
and Army of Occupation
# War Diary
France, Belgium and Germany

66 DIVISION
198 Infantry Brigade
Lancashire Fusiliers
12th Battalion
1 July 1918 - 31 July 1918

WO95/3140/4

The Naval & Military Press Ltd
www.nmarchive.com
Published in association with The National Archives

Published by

## The Naval & Military Press Ltd

Unit 10 Ridgewood Industrial Park,

Uckfield, East Sussex,

TN22 5QE England

Tel: +44 (0) 1825 749494

www.naval-military-press.com

www.nmarchive.com

*This diary has been reprinted in facsimile from the original. Any imperfections are inevitably reproduced and the quality may fall short of modern type and cartographic standards.*

© **Crown Copyright**
**Images reproduced by permission of The National Archives, London, England, 2015.**

# Contents

| Document type | Place/Title | Date From | Date To |
|---|---|---|---|
| Heading | WO95/3140/4 | | |
| Heading | 66 Div 198 Bde 12 Bn Lancs Fus 1918 July Only Obsorbed By B Bn From Salonika 22 Div 165 Bde | | |
| War Diary | La Marrain | 01/07/1918 | 02/07/1918 |
| War Diary | Sarigol | 02/07/1918 | 02/07/1918 |
| War Diary | Sa Marrain | 02/07/1918 | 02/07/1918 |
| War Diary | Sarigol | 02/07/1918 | 06/07/1918 |
| War Diary | On The Line | 05/07/1918 | 06/07/1918 |
| War Diary | Itea | 07/07/1918 | 07/07/1918 |
| War Diary | On The Above | 08/07/1918 | 16/07/1918 |
| War Diary | Serquex | 17/07/1918 | 22/07/1918 |
| War Diary | Haudricourt Camp | 23/07/1918 | 25/07/1918 |
| War Diary | Haudricourt | 25/07/1918 | 31/07/1918 |
| Operation(al) Order(s) | 12th Lancashire Fusiliers Order No.14 | 01/07/1918 | 01/07/1918 |
| Operation(al) Order(s) | 12th Lancashire Fusiliers Order No.15 | 04/07/1918 | 04/07/1918 |
| Miscellaneous | 12th Lancashire Fusiliers Circular Memorandum No.4 | 29/07/1918 | 29/07/1918 |
| Heading | Cover For Documents. Confidential War Diary of 12th (S) Bn Lancashire Fusiliers from 1-7-18 to 31-7-18 | | |

WO 95/3140/4

66 DIV
198 BDE

12 BN LANCS FUS

1918 JULY only

Absorbed by 6 BN

FROM SALONIKA
2 BN: 165 BDE

# WAR DIARY
## or
## INTELLIGENCE SUMMARY.
(Erase heading not required.)

Army Form C. 2118.

| Place | Date | Hour | Summary of Events and Information | Remarks and references to Appendices |
|---|---|---|---|---|
| | 2/7/16 | | [illegible handwritten entry regarding parties, officers, SARIGOL etc.] | |
| SARIGOL | 3/7/16 | | Weather fine. Battalion noting & re-equipping. The men are accommodated in huts & the general arrangements are quite good. All the officers in mess at the SARIGOL Hotel which is quite close to camp. | |
| | 4/7/16 | | Weather fine. Battalion noting. As the officers were so busy passed through the gas chamber. The C in C inspected the Battalion in Light Marching Order at 1800 hours. The Battalion | |

| Place | Date | Hour | Summary of Events and Information | Remarks and references to Appendices |
|---|---|---|---|---|
| SARIGOL | 4/7/18 | | were drawn up in mass & the C in C carefully inspected all ranks after the inspection all the officers & W.O's were formed up in front of the C in C who had each one good-bye afterwards presenting the Ribbon of the "Military Cross" to Capt. F. Franks & the Ribbon of the "Meritorious Service Medal" to the said P. Ferguson A.S.C. late C.Q.M.S. of this Battalion. The Battalion were then closed up & the C in C made the following speech:- "Lancashire Fusiliers. Before you leave this country I want to thank you officially for the excellent work done and the magnificent discipline you have maintained during the time you have been out here. I know that at one time you suffered from influenza more than any other Regiment, but I am sorry glad to see how | |

# WAR DIARY
## or
## INTELLIGENCE SUMMARY.

Army Form C. 2118.

| Place | Date | Hour | Summary of Events and Information | Remarks and references to Appendices |
|---|---|---|---|---|
| SARIGOL | 4/7/16 | | "and you are looking now. You are going to France because your Own Cavl: troops the West-Lancashire Division has suffered even loses and need reinforcements. You are going as a Battalion, to take the place of other Battalion that have been practically wiped out, but the same spirit that has been shown by the splendid troops in France, the always been shown by the Lancashire troops in this country. I congratulate you on it. I am very sorry you are going but it is for the good of the country." Order to move the APPENDIX ☓ Water Jars 6" 340 & 1 pt. | |
| SARIGOL | 5/7/16 | | entrained at 2.9.65 hrs, the train left SARIGOL at 2.9.15 hrs for BRALO. Arrived SUYLAR, EKATERINI, LARISSA DEMERDJI-DEMIRLI-BRALO 6.8.30 hrs. The Companies detrained at BRALO marched | |

# WAR DIARY or INTELLIGENCE SUMMARY

Army Form C. 2118.

| Place | Date | Hour | Summary of Events and Information | Remarks and references to Appendices |
|---|---|---|---|---|
| On a hill | 6/7/16 | | At the Rest Camp when a "bull" of about 60 was reported to the men at 10.15. Rumour the Half Battalion entrained on a fund ferry Convoy & moved to ITEA when we arrived about 16.30 hours. | |
| ITEA | 7/7/16 | | Battles fire apart from plenty of artillery passes the men had nothing to do all day & in line sun are much too weary. Everyone shows they were just happy enjoying themselves & most of the afternoon spent sleeping at 19.30 & again at 22.30 we had news the English other half Battalion would be concentrated & 19.30 & 21.30 & the whole half Battalion arrived at 19.30. Hours appointed are for Camp. | |

# WAR DIARY or INTELLIGENCE SUMMARY

Army Form C. 2118.

(Erase heading not required.)

Instructions regarding War Diaries and Intelligence Summaries are contained in F. S. Regs., Part II. and the Staff Manual respectively. Title pages will be prepared in manuscript.

| Place | Date | Hour | Summary of Events and Information | Remarks and references to Appendices |
|---|---|---|---|---|
| On the march | 8/7/18 | | Weather fine. The Battalion left the Rest Camp at 0500 hours & entrained on the TIMGAD at 0600 hours. The boat sailed at 0830 hours & the journey to TARTO – which was accomplished without incident – ended at 0700 hours of 9ᵗʰ inst. | |
| | 9/7/18 | | Until 0930 hours that the Battalion commenced to disembark & that was only one lighter available it was not until 1135 hours that the whole were clear of the ship. The Battalion moved into the Rest Camp. The men were encamped in & near it. On arrival we were given to understand that the Battalion would not entrain the journey before the 13ᵗʰ inst. but at 1930 hours orders were received that we were to entrain at ST THING station – which was only about 50 yards from the bivouac – at 1015 inst. | |

# WAR DIARY
## or
## INTELLIGENCE SUMMARY.
*(Erase heading not required.)*

Army Form C. 2118.

| Place | Date | Hour | Summary of Events and Information | Remarks and references to Appendices |
|---|---|---|---|---|
| On the O.M. | 10/9/18 | | Weather fine. The Battalion entrained at CIMINO station at 04.15 hours on the 10th inst. & the train moved off at 05.05 hours. The men were accommodated 30 in a truck. The senior officer & men were accompanied by the senior Italian officer to an early compartment. The first stop of importance was BRINDISI where a halt of two hours was made & the men had tea & a wash. Further stops for tea & additional purposes were made at the following places. BARRESA at 18.00 hours 10th inst. FOGGIA at 07.00 hours 11th inst. PESCARA at 19.00 hours 11th inst. FAENZA at 09.00 hours 12th inst. SAVONA at 09.30 hours 13th inst. TORINO at 17.15 13th inst. (The Italian Lunch ration was served at 18.45 hours 13th inst.) MIRAMAS at 08.30 hours 14th inst. LE TEIL at [illegible] inst. PARAY-LE-MONIAL at 05.30 hours | |

# WAR DIARY
## or
## INTELLIGENCE SUMMARY.

Army Form C. 2118.

| Place | Date | Hour | Summary of Events and Information | Remarks and references to Appendices |
|---|---|---|---|---|
| On the move | 10/7/18 | | 15th inst. No further stop was made until we reached our destination – FORGES-LES-EAUX at 1325 15th inst. The Battalion detrained & after the men had had some food we commenced the march to SERQUEUX Camp & arrived there at 1630 hrs. | ff |
| SERQUEUX | 17/7/18 | | Weather stormy. Battalion making & cleaning accoutrements etc. The Camp Officer inspected the Camp at 1300 hours & one present N.C.O. was sent to U.K. | ff |
| " | 18/7/18 | | Weather stormy. Battalion Cadre finishing generally cleaning up. Capt. Wilthorpe 'B' Coy & S.O.R. proceeded on leave to U.K. 24"/ & lifted 'C' was admitted to hospital | ff |
| " | 19/7/18 | | Weather stormy. Battalion carrying out Musketry. B.F.P.T. Drill under Company arrangements from 0800 – 1000 hrs. | ff |

Army Form C. 2118.

# WAR DIARY
## or
## INTELLIGENCE SUMMARY.
(Erase heading not required.)

| Place | Date | Hour | Summary of Events and Information | Remarks and references to Appendices |
|---|---|---|---|---|
| SERQUEUX | 19/7/18 | | Specialist training under Specialist Officers. The Battalion on loftier mud filth at recent. The sick rate is falling. 2/Lt C. JACKSON & 3. O.R. proceeded on leave to U.K. | ff. |
| " | 20/7/18 | | Weather fine. Battalion Route Marching & Specialist training. 4. O.R. proceeded on leave to U.K. Capt. N.V. Lowe Young Battalion visiting Brigadier General | ff. |
| " | 21/7/18 | | Weather dull & stormy. Battalion resting. Brigadier Gen. G.C. WILLIAMS D.S.O. inspected Camp at 1800 hours. 198th Inf. Bde. Order S/3/101 received. H. O.R. proceeded on leave to U.S. | ff. |
| " | 22/7/18 | | Weather fine. The Battalion proceeded to HAUDRICOURT in accordance with 198th Bde Order OB 101 & marched into a Camp just N of the village. The march commenced at 0830 hours & the Battalion arrived in new camps at 1330 hours | ff. |

# WAR DIARY or INTELLIGENCE SUMMARY

Army Form C. 2118.

| Place | Date | Hour | Summary of Events and Information | Remarks and references to Appendices |
|---|---|---|---|---|
| HAUDRICOURT Camp | 23/7/18 | | Weather stormy. The Battalion noting generally cleaning up & special orders carried out during under their respective Specialist Officers. Major C.E. Gutmer & Lt G.B.C. Hollin & 6 O.R. to U.K. on leave. | |
| | 24/7/18 | | Weather stormy. Battalion working training as follows:- "A" & "D" Coys each 1 Officer 3 Sergts & 60 O.R. working on mess Rifle Range near ST VALERY from: 0800–1200 "A" Coy. 1300–1700 "D" Coy. "B" & "C" Coys each 1 Officer & 50 O.R. working 1200 "D" Coy." "B" & "C" Coys each 1 Officer & 50 O.R. working on Bombardment Pits in Camp in two reliefs 0800-1200 & 1200-1600 hours. Specialist continued their training. 4 O.R. to U.K. on leave. | |
| | 25/7/18 | | Weather stormy. Battalion working training as follows:- "A" Company General Training under Coy Comdr. "B" Company Route Marching. "C" & D working on Rifle range. Bombardment | |

# WAR DIARY
## or
## INTELLIGENCE SUMMARY.

*(Erase heading not required.)*

Army Form C. 2118.

| Place | Date | Hour | Summary of Events and Information | Remarks and references to Appendices |
|---|---|---|---|---|
| HAUBRICOURT | 25/7/18 | | Bn in camp. Specialists continued training. 4 O.R. to U.K. on leave | ff |
| " " | 26/7/18 | | Weather overcast with light rainfall at intervals. The Battalion working training. The Brigade Commander visited camp. | ff |
| | | | 4 O.R. proceeded on leave to U.K. | |
| " " | 27/7/18 | | Weather stormy. The Battalion working training. Capt. J.W. Deane & 3 O.R. proceeded to U.K. on leave | ff |
| " " | 28/7/18 | | Weather fine. The Battalion ruling. The Battalion attended Divine Service C of E at 1000 hours. Lt. P. Tyson & 3 O.R. proceeded to U.K. on leave | ff |
| " " | 29/7/18 | | Weather fine with sunshine all day. The Battalion working training. 4 O.R. proceeded to U.K. on leave. | ff |

Copy of B H issued at 1000 hr. See APPENDIX 3 attached

# WAR DIARY
## or
## INTELLIGENCE SUMMARY.

Army Form C. 2118.

Instructions regarding War Diaries and Intelligence Summaries are contained in F. S. Regs., Part II. and the Staff Manual respectively. Title pages will be prepared in manuscript.

(Erase heading not required.)

| Place | Date | Hour | Summary of Events and Information | Remarks and references to Appendices |
|---|---|---|---|---|
| HAVRINCOURT | 30/7/18 | | Weather fine. Battalion training running & P.T. in Rear. | |
| " | 31/7/18 | | Weather fine, bright sunshine all day. The Battalion working parties. The G.O.C. 199th Bde. inspected the Battalion Transport at 10.00 hours & expressed himself well pleased. The general turn out. In addition Group parties gave a performance in camp at 2.30 p.m. In the afternoon. Whippet off during the past month we as follows:- 3 Officers & 64. O.R. 5. O.R. killed & O.R. on leave. | |

2nd August 1918

R. J. Smith(?)
Lieut Colonel
Comdg 13th/18th Lancashire Fusiliers

SECRET

## 12th LANCASHIRE FUSILIERS ORDER No.14.

APPENDIX I

Copy No. 2
1st July 1918.

1. The Battalion will move to SARIGOL on the night 2nd/3rd July 1918 as follows :-

   (a) Battalion Headquarters, "A", "B" and "C" Companies will proceed in three Motor Lorry convoys (of 11 lorries each) as per time table below.

   (b) "D" Company, less 1 Officer with Lewis Guns and detachment, and all baggage, will travel by train. O.C "D" Company will report to the R.T.O., CUGUNCI at 00.15 hours 3rd July 1918, and will proceed by train No. 202 leaving CUGUNCI at 01.00 hours, 3rd July 1918, arriving SARIGOL 02.35 hours.

   (c) The 1st Line Transport under the Transport Officer will march via JANES to SARIGOL. Formation, three echelons, at ten minutes interval, starting at 17.00 hours.

2. TIME TABLE: LORRY CONVOYS.

| Company | Time  | Lorries | Remarks |
|---------|-------|---------|---------|
| Bn.H.Q. | 17.30 | 6       | Not more than 20 men will travel in each lorry. |
| "A"     | "     | 5       | Men will wear full equipment, less pack. |
| "A"     | 18.30 | 4       |  |
| "B"     | "     | 7       | Packs, blankets, bivouacs and nets will be taken in the lorries with the men and used as seats. |
| "B"     | 19.30 | 1       |  |
| "C"     | "     | 8       |  |
| "D"     | "     | 2       | One lorry per Company will be used for the Lewis Guns and all Company baggage. |

3. Convoy duties :-
   Capt R.A.V.White will be i/c of the 17.30 hours convoy.
   Capt I.S.Rutherford          "       "  18.30    "       "
   Capt P.Lockett               "       "  19.30    "       "

   On arrival at SARIGOL the Officer i/c each lorry convoy will report to the Administrative Commandant for further instructions.

4. All baggage will be stacked, by Companies, near the road 40 yards N of the Guard room by 16.00 hours.

5.   The Battalion will be clear of the present camp by 17.00 hours, Companies will move out and pile arms on the Football ground and then return to clean up the camp.

6.   Rations for consumption on the 3rd July will be drawn at SARIGOL.

7.   O.C Companies will render to Battalion Headquarters by 12.00 hours 4th July 1918 a nominal roll in duplicate of all ranks proceeding with their Companies, including Battalion Headquarters and Transport

Issued at 2200 hours.

J. Franks
Captain,
Adjutant, 12th Bn Lancashire Fusiliers.

Copies to :-
1 File.
2 War Diary.
3 A. Company.
4 B. ,,
5 C. ,,
6 D. ,,
7 Transport Officer.
8 Quartermaster.
9 Spare.

SECRET

12th LANCASHIRE FUSILIERS ORDER No. 15.

APPENDIX 2

Copy No..2
4th July 1918.

1. The Battalion will move to ORALO on the 5th and 6th July 1918 in accordance with following time-table:-
TIME-TABLE.

| Date. | Companies. | Hour of Entraining and Place. | Hour of Departure. | Remarks. |
|---|---|---|---|---|
| 5th. | Bn. H.Q. "A" & "D" Coys. | 07.30 hours, Ground N of Camp. | 09.15 | Dress; Full Marching Order, less pack. The men will carry their pack and blankets and use them as seats in the trucks. |
| 6th. | "B" & "C" Coys. Transport. | 07.30 hours, Ground N of Camp. | 09.15 | |

Major C.E.GARDNER will be O.C Train on the 6th inst, and
2nd Lieut R.F.HINSON will be Train Adjutant.
C.S.M. BARNES will be Train Sergt. Major.
R.C.M.S. AINSWORTH will be Train C.M.Sergt.

2. BAGGAGE.

   (a) All baggage will be stacked near the road in front of the Q.M. Stores, by 06.45 hours on the 5th and 6th respectively.

   (b) Each Company will detail a loading party of 1 N.C.O., and 16 men to load the baggage on to the Motor lorries at 06.50 hours.

   (c) Each Company will detail an Officer and 20 O.R to report to the R.T.O. BARIGOL at 07.30 hours to load the baggage on to the train. This party will take their equipment and packs with them.

3. RATIONS.

Only one day's rations are carried on the train, and these are in the usual way held by each individual except:-

(a) Tea, Sugar and Milk ration for the whole of the details on the train will be placed in charge of the Train C.M.Sergt., and handed in bulk on arrival at LARISSA (where a halt of 1 hour is made) to the R.T.O. who will have tea prepared in advance.

(b) Two Orderlies will be detailed per coach or wagon to report to the Cookhouse immediately after the train has arrived at the station, for tea.

(c) Dixies of tea will be supplied to the Orderlies detailed - these will be returned to the Cookhouse 10 minutes before the departure of the train.

(d) All men except the abovementioned orderlies, will be forbidden to visit the Cookhouse, and the Train guard will be posted to see that this order is rigidly enforced.

4. WATER.

Water bottles will be carried filled and this water will be looked upon as a reserve in case of emergency. As the purity of the water supplies at EKATERINI, LARISSA and LIANACLADI is very doubtful, no Officer, N.C.O. or man will drink any water other than that which has been either chlorinated or boiled; supplies of which are available at EKATERINI and LARISSA Stations.

---

5. DISCIPLINE.

(a) A senior N.C.O. will be placed in charge of each coach or wagon and he will at once make a list of all men in his coach. This N.C.O. will detail two Corporals, one on each side of the coach or wagon, to assist him in carrying out the Train Orders.

(b) No N.C.O. or man will get out of their carriage on the left side of the train (in the direction of PIAIO) except at EKATERINI and LARISSA.

---

6. GUARDS.

Two guards for the train, each consisting of 1 Officer and 12 O.R. One of these guards will be located in the brake van at one end of the train, and the other guard with the Officers kits will be located in the goods wagon at the opposite end of the train.

The Company Orderly Officer will be the Officer i/c the guard. The guards will remain armed and equipped throughout their period of duty.

NOTE :- The fact that the Brake Van is occupied by British personnel is not to preclude Railway Officials from entering or travelling in the van.

On arrival at an authorised stopping places, the guards will detrain as soon as the train stops, and will see that instructions in para (7) are complied with.

---

7. GENERAL DUTIES OF GUARD.

(a) No N.C.O. or man is allowed to leave the train without permission.

(b) No unauthorised persons are permitted to enter the train.

(c) When the O.C Train considers there is sufficient time to allow men to leave the train, he will give orders accordingly and post sentries on exits, refreshment rooms, etc., and also on all latrines to warn men when the time is drawing near for departure.

(d) The guards will see that the men do not straggle and will be responsible that they do not leave the Station premises on any pretext. Men will not be allowed to enter any refreshment room.

(e) All men will be warned of the length of the halt, and ordered to parade outside their carriages five minutes before the train is due to start.

(f) All ranks will be forbidden to travel on the top of, or on the steps of a vehicle. No Officer, N.C.O. or man is allowed to travel on the engine, or in the Brake Van except the guard detailed in para. 6.

8. ABSENTEES.

Before the train leaves any halt or station, the Officer in charge of each party will assure himself that all men are on board, and will report to the O.C Train to this effect.
In the event of any man being missing, the O.C.Train will report the name, number and Regiment of the man to the R.T.O.at the de-training station, stating if possible, where the man was left.

9. WINES, ETC.

No wine, spirits or beer may be purchased during the journey.

10. RAILWAY STAFF.

Officers and other ranks travelling on the train are on no account permitted to interfere with the Railway working, or with the Railway Staff in the execution of their duty.

11. MEDICAL ARRANGEMENTS.

(a) Sergt HUNTINGDON with half the Medical equipment will travel with Battalion Headquarters on the 5th. A Medical Officer for duty on board train to BRALO for the first half of the Battalion will join the train at DUDULAR.
(b) The Medical Officer with the other half of the Medical equipment will travel with the second half of the Battalion on the 6th inst.

12. REFRESHMENTS AND ACCOMMODATION.

(a) EKATERINI. - A Y.M.C.A. Tent is provided at this halt where tea is served free to soldiers desiring it; it is located on LEFT of Station in direction of BRALO. Men will get out on this side and be formed up under their Officers and marched in file to the Cookhouse; each man carrying his Mess-tin. - After receiving Tea men can break off and purchase anything they require at the Y.M.C.A Tent. Instructions as to their being ready to detrain at EKATERINI with Mess Tins must be issued to men before arrival at this Station.
(b) DERELY. - A Y.M.C.A. Tent is provided at this Station and is located on the RIGHT of Station in direction of BRALO.

13. LATRINE ACCOMMODATION.

Latrine accommodation is provided for troops at the following stations :-

   EKATERINI. - On the right hand side of the Railway in the direction of SALONICA.

   LARISSA  -  -do-    -do-    -do-

   LIONACLADI  -di-    -do-    -do-

   DEMILE -    (Under construction)

14. These Orders will be read out on parade and carefully explained to all ranks prior to entraining.

Copies to :- File
          War Diary
          Major Gardner.
          A. Company
          B. ,,
          C. ,,
          D. ,,
          Transport Officer

Captain,
Adjutant, 12th Lanc. Fusiliers.

Quartermaster.
Spare.

12th Lancashire Fusiliers.    Circular Memorandum
                                        No 4
29th July 1918.

## Training.

1. Companies will train during the week ending 3rd August 1918 as follows:—

    Training Programme.

| Coys. | Date. | Area. | Hours of Training. | Remarks. |
|---|---|---|---|---|
| D. | 30th | A.1. | 0800-1200 | For this week the 4 hours Training will include the time taken in going to and from the Training Area. |
| A. |  | A.2. | -- -- |  |
| B. | 31st | C.1. | -- -- |  |
| C. | " | C.2. | -- -- |  |
| D. | 2nd. | B.1. | -- -- |  |
| A. |  | B.2. | -- -- |  |
| B. | 3rd. | B.1. | -- -- |  |
| C. |  | B.2. | -- -- |  |

2. Allotment of S.A.A. Grenades etc.

    The allotment of S.A.A. Grenades etc, is as follows:—

| Coy. | S.A.A. | No 23 Hand. | No 23 Rifle. | No 36 Rifle. | No 34 Rifle. |
|---|---|---|---|---|---|
| A. | 4,000 | 3 | 30 | 16 | 3 |
| B. | 4,000 | 3 | 30 | 16 | 3 |
| C. | 4,000 | 3 | 30 | 16 | 4 |
| D. | 4,000 | 3 | 30 | 16 | 4 |
| H.Q. L.G's. | 10,000 | — | — | — | — |

3. Special attention will be paid to the following points in training:—

    (a) **Musketry:** This will include rapid loading and firing, fire control and direction, and recognition of targets. Care will be taken that the men adopt the correct positions when firing.

    (b) **Gas Instruction.** Every use will be made of the Gas N.C.O. to give instruction in gas drill, and Companies will also be practised in training whilst wearing the box respirator.

    (c) **Bayonet Fighting, P.T. & Recreational Games.** will be practised daily.

    (d) **Drill.** Close-Order Drill together with handling of arms and saluting with and without arms will be practised daily.

Circular Memorandum No 4,   Sheet 2.   9/7/18.

(e) **Platoon Training.** Platoons organised in three sections complete in L. Guns (which for the present will be obtained from the Companies not training) will be practised in extended order, and in the adoption of formations suitable to ground and fire.

(f) **Bombs.** As soon as bombs are available every man will practise throwing at least two live bombs.

(g) **Ranges.** When B2 Area is allotted to a Company every advantage will be taken of the range to carry out Short Range practices. Targets for this purpose will be found in the shed on the Range. Companies using the Range will be responsible for the repairing of the targets.

4. **Signallers.** The signallers will be given instruction in musketry, including firing on the range, during the next two weeks.

5. **Classes of Instruction.** The following classes of instruction will be carried on daily:-

| | | |
|---|---|---|
| Lewis Gunners, | under | 2/Lt C. W. Jones. M.M. |
| Signallers, | under | 2/Lt R. F. Hinson. |
| Scouts, | under | 2/Lt P. Baker. |

6. **Tactical Schemes.** Tactical schemes will be worked out on the ground by Officers & N.C.Os during each week of the training. The tactical schemes will be continuous, but divided into phases. Each phase will first be worked out by Coy Commanders with the Commanding Officer on the ground. Subsequently Coy Commanders will work out on the ground the further details with their Platoon and Section leaders.
The day and time on which Coy Commanders are carrying out these exercises will be notified to Bn. H. Q.

7. **Riding Classes.** A riding class consisting of 8 Officers per Battalion will take place daily under the Bde V.O. Classes will assemble at Bde H.Q at 1500 hours. The names of the officers selected to attend this course will be notified later.

8. **Inspections.** The Commanding Officer will inspect Companies in Fighting Order as follows:-

| Coy. | Date. | Time. |
|---|---|---|
| "B" | 31st | 1430 hours |
| "A" | 2nd | ---- |
| "C" | 3rd | ---- |
| "D" | 5th | ---- |

9. **Watches.** All watches will be synchronised at the Orderly Room at 0730 hours daily.

Issued at: 1000 hrs
Copies to:
"A" Coy 1     Lewis Gun O. 6
"B"    2      Scout O. 7
"C"    3      File. 8
"D"    4      War Diary. 9
Signalling Of. 5

Army Form W. 3091.

# Cover for Documents.

### Nature of Enclosures.

CONFIDENTIAL

WAR DIARY

OF

12th (S) Bn LANCASHIRE FUSILIERS

From 1. 7. 18. to 31. 7. 18.

R. Strife, Lt Colonel
COMDG. 12th. BN. LANC. FUS.

---

### Notes, or Letters written.

www.ingramcontent.com/pod-product-compliance
Lightning Source LLC
Chambersburg PA
CBHW081508160426
43193CB00014B/2616